W9-DHR-703

Country Baskets

By Don & Carol Raycraft

Published by

WALLACE-HOMESTEAD BOOK CO.
P. O. BOX BI
DES MOINES, IOWA 50304

ACKNOWLEDGMENT

The authors thank "The Rookery A.A." for assistance in preparing this book.

Photography by
Tpv
Ron Hayes and Bruce Benedict
Deposit, New York

Third Printing, 1980

Library of Congress Catalog Card Number 75-38390
ISBN: 0-87069-146-5

Country Baskets

In the October 1975 issue of the Maine Antique Digest, Joan Kindler describes the climb of American stoneware out of the antiques' basement to a position of respectability among collectors. Painted furniture, samplers, quilts, and weathervanes have also been discovered by collectors in recent years, and their prices have multiplied several times.

Now, American country baskets are climbing the basement stairs. Their prices are increasing dramatically, and the demand for them is growing rapidly outside the cult of searchers who have appreciated them for years.

The impetus in basket collecting began in the early 1900s with the establishment of The Basket Fraternity by George W. James. James and his organization were concerned with the study and construction of American Indian baskets.

In 1903, Otis Mason and the Smithsonian Institution produced a landmark study of Indian baskets that is still a primary research tool for collectors. The work by Mason and The Basket Fraternity was a significant part of a large-scale craft revival in the first decade of the twentieth century.

Formation of the Society for the Preservation of New England Antiquities in 1910 further increased awareness of the nation's heritage in furniture, pottery, and textiles through both Society publications and local organizations.

The founding of Antiques magazine in 1922 by Homer Eaton Keyes provided for the first time a national publication that combined scholarly articles with well-illustrated advertisements from dealers all over the country. While other facets of early American life were being explored and documented by origin, maker, and date, basketry was ignored. Rarely did Antiques or the other publications that followed over the next 50 years publish articles on this oldest American craft.

Unusual split drying basket, circa 1840

Plate 1

The two baskets on the barnboard wall illustrate two types of American basketry. The large, handcrafted, circular basket is said to have been used for drying herbs and mushrooms. Baskets of this type are difficult to date because construction methods and materials changed very little over nearly 100 years. The factory-made willow basket, a product of the late 1800s, probably had no specific purpose.

Early baskets were constructed with utility in mind. Decoration had little place in small-town or back-country America. Time was as scarce as money, and the baskets that were made and bartered by traveling basketmakers were used daily rather than displayed with the family pewter or china.

The three split oak baskets on the bench are typical of the handcrafted products of the period from the 1860s through the early 1900s.

Plate 2

The split basket on the Shaker dry sink was used for a variety of purposes. The handcrafted field basket at the bottom right was valuable for carrying produce from the garden to the kitchen. Locally made baskets bear tool marks and feature irregularities in size and design that factory-made products do not possess.

The open tray was a late factory-made basket used to carry flowers and cuttings from the yard and garden.

Note the variation in the handles of the three baskets on the brick floor. The unique twisted handle on the large kidney basket was designed for extra strength. The split oak handle on the tray was made on a veneer machine and fastened to the body of the basket with nails. The carved handle on the field basket carries the typical tool marks and imperfections.

Baskets sold as "old" should show distinct signs of use and abuse. The oak splits may be frayed or cracked, and holes in the basket are not uncommon. Even casual collectors should be wary of early baskets in perfect condition.

Plate 3

Baskets have been made from all types of plants, leaves, grasses, vines, and roots. The two large stick baskets are contemporary pottery carriers from Mexico. Redware flower pots are transported to the United States in baskets similar to these. The twigs are bound with twine and appear to be considerably more ancient than they are. We purchased these baskets for $5 each from a local plant shop owner. He was amazed that anyone would be interested in them and indicated that he routinely disposed of them like most packing materials.

In recent years there has been an influx of baskets, pine furniture, kitchen utensils, and iron lighting and fireplace equipment from Mexico. These items show considerable wear and give every indication of being from the early 1800s. In fact, they are purchased in rural areas where they are still in use, imported to the United States, and sold as New England antiques.

Plate 4

The large rectangular basket made of maple and hickory was used for displaying bread on the counter in a late 1800s grocery store.

The size of the handcrafted split field basket at the bottom left is unusual. It was constructed by placing weavers (quarter-inch-wide split oak strands) repeatedly over and under larger split oak stakes or ribs.

The wicker (willow) garden basket at the center top was factory-made in the early 1900s. Wicker was enormously popular in making furniture and a wide range of household goods during this period. Wicker baskets are commonly found today.

The woven egg basket in the center was constructed much like the larger field basket and has a hickory handle double-wrapped into the sides of the basket.

The factory-made basket of ash on the walnut chopping block has a solid wood bottom. Its handle is nailed to the sides of the basket. Wood bottoms were used in baskets designed to carry heavy loads and are uncommon. They often were used to replace worn split bottoms.

Factory-made split laundry basket, circa 1920 to 1930

Plate 5

The wicker (willow) storage basket at the right is a contemporary example of a common product of the late 1800s and early 1900s. Its size and design are similar to the earlier baskets. With use it will be impossible to distinguish it from the earlier baskets.

The large woven laundry basket of split oak dates from the 1920s. It contains the nails and metal rivets commonly found on baskets of this period. The handle is a two-inch slice of machine-cut split.

The laundry basket is of the quality that can be purchased almost anywhere for a few dollars. Its value will probably never increase much because it has no unique or attractive features in design or style. A collector interested in baskets of this type should seek examples in perfect condition.

Ryegrass basket and late plaited basket of split oak

Plate 6

The basket containing the butter molds and the basket on the seat of the early chair table are made of ryegrass. Both were constructed by a simple coiling process in which progressively larger coils of ryegrass are made and bound with thin strips of hickory. The baskets were used in baking and for storing small food items. For example, kneaded dough wrapped in linen was placed in the baskets and allowed to rise. Rye baskets are more commonly found in Pennsylvania, Ohio, and New York than in other sections of the country.

The painted basket is a late all-purpose example constructed by a process called plaiting. A form of braiding, plaiting involves the interweaving of two strands of split in an over and under pattern. Unlike weaving, plaiting does not use stakes or ribs in the construction of a basket.

*Unusually large herb gathering basket (the
Rookery A.A. Collection)*

Plate 7

The exceptionally large basket, possibly Shaker in origin, was used in gathering herbs. A basket of this size is difficult to integrate into a collection and display in a home. The basket has a series of supports on the inside and outside to provide additional strength. The rim of this particular basket is doublewrapped, as is the oval basket at the center left, which dates from the late 1700s. Both baskets have a plaited rather than woven bottom.

The double-handled market basket at the lower right has green strips finely woven into the sides. Midwestern collectors seldom find early baskets decorated with dyed split, paint, or colorful stenciled decorations.

The miniature assen basket and the handleless plaited basket with stenciled sides are both unusual.

Variety of early woven baskets (The Rook-
ery A.A. Collection)

Plate 8

These early handcrafted baskets were constructed to serve a variety of purposes. They date from the early 1800s. Each is tightly woven from split and has a double-wrapped rim.

A collector should attempt to secure as many different basket forms as possible. Some especially interesting forms are difficult to use in homes because of their unwieldy size. However, handled baskets, which can be found in numerous forms, are rather easily used.

Some early basketmakers made sets or nests of baskets in various sizes, but most or all of these have long since been broken up. A complete set would truly be a rare find today.

Field basket, Indian basket, and open basket (The Rookery A.A. Collection)

Plate 9

The large field or orchard basket has a plaited bottom of uncommonly wide split. It was used for gathering apples or vegetables in the early 1800s.

The finely woven open basket has inset handles and green, red, and blue split decoration.

The open split basket dates from the early 1800s and has a double-wrapped rim.

We have been searching for baskets since the late 1960s and have been amazed at the steady increase in prices at antique shows and in shops. Recently we were told of an unusual basket in what was supposed to be an antique shop in a nearby Illinois town. Surrounded by Mrs. Butterworth bottles and stainless steel meat grinders was the rarest basket we now have in our collection.

Plate 10

The large basket, used to store goose down for pillows and bed covers, is particularly unusual because it has its original lid. The lid is made from split and ryegrass. The split on the body of the basket is also colored and stenciled.

The dome-top basket on the chair is also uncommon. It contains wide split and the remains of an original stenciled decoration.

The square basket has a flat lid and a checkerboard pattern of colored split.

Plate 11

The unusual twig work basket at the top left was used to transport heavy loads. Constructed of willow twigs and hickory split, it is crudely made but an excellent example of an early basket form. In fact, the basket's crudeness and pure functionality make it almost classic in design.

Bark was left on the twigs used in baskets designed for work outdoors. Willow used in making baskets for storing and serving food inside the home had the bark removed before construction.

The stave basket bound with wire was used in gathering hops. It dates from the mid-1800s.

The half-bushel basket with handles, a classic basket form, dates from the 1700s. Its rim is double-wrapped with oak split.

The oval basket on the floor served a function similar to the twig work basket. This basket was used to carry fruit from the orchard, vegetables from the garden, and shelled corn or wheat from the grainery. Both it and the twig work basket were handcrafted in the mid-1800s.

Plate 12

This variety of baskets is from the collections of Mr. and Mrs. T. O. Dawson and Dr. and Mrs. B. H. Robbins, Jr., of Champaign, Illinois.

The buttocks basket at the far right is fairly typical in size. It was constructed in the Midwest. Seldom do collectors find very small or large buttocks baskets. Small baskets may be 4 to 6 inches wide. Larger examples range from 2 to 3 feet wide.

The factory-made wicker (willow) basket and the hand-crafted willow basket from the late 1800s present an interesting comparison. The factory-made wicker baskets were tightly woven with each twig precisely cut and shaped by machine. In the case of the handcrafted baskets, dried willow twigs were loosely woven to split oak or hickory ribs. These baskets were used for gathering flowers, fruits, or vegetables.

Photograph by Ms. Bonnie Dawson

Variety of early decorated baskets (The Rookery A.A. Collection)

Plate 13

American country baskets are often found with freehand painted designs, stenciled decoration, or multicolored split in various patterns. This variety of decorated baskets is from the 1800s.

The large open basket on the top shelf was painted with freehand stars and dots and also stenciled. Some early decorators used a sectioned potato dipped in paint when they stenciled baskets rather than the more conventional cut stencil.

The tiny berry basket on the second shelf is decorated with red, yellow, and blue paint.

Baskets found with remnants of the original decoration should generally be left alone. Attempts to refinish early baskets should also be avoided. The best finish for a basket is the original one.

The small basket on the bottom shelf is lined with wallpaper and was used as a container for powdered herbs or dried blossoms.

Variety of baskets from New York State Antiques Shop (Foreman's Folly, Worcester, New York)

Plate 14

The collector who visits the antique shop on the corner or several miles down the road may happen on many of these basket forms. Wicker, split oak, American Indian, and various types of straw baskets are still being found all over the country. Factory-made baskets from the 1880 to 1930 golden age of wicker and rice straw tend to predominate. Rice straw or Chinee baskets were manufactured in the Orient and imported in vast quantities for use as sewing baskets, display on knick-knack shelves, and as prizes at canasta parties.

The collector looking for early basket forms is probably best advised to limit his search to antique shops that stock early pottery, textiles, painted furniture, ironware, and woodenware.

Unusual rye baskets, circa 1860

Plate 15

The decorative possibilities for country baskets in an early American setting are obvious. Dried flowers, gourds, fruits, and vegetables in baskets add considerable warmth to any home.

Perhaps the most unusual baskets in this picture are the two rye baskets. We purchased the hickory-handled rye basket on the Shaker chair in the late 1960s. At that particular time, baskets were inexpensive and held in little regard by most collectors. It is the only rye basket with a handle we have seen.

The large rye basket to the right of the Shaker desk probably was used for indoor storage of potatoes, apples, and nuts. Rye baskets occasionally were used outdoors as bee's nests.

Two uncommon split baskets, circa 1850

Plate 16

The split basket at the left is unusual because of its small size and flat back. When this particular basket was purchased, it supposedly was used in gathering eggs. The flat back allows it to be hung against a wall and used for storage. Its size limits the number of eggs it could hold.

The larger basket appears to be in an original condition. It is footed and could have been used for storage. Footed baskets are uncommon. They were used in the Midwest for storing potatoes and onions in underground root cellars.

Both baskets are woven of split and contain oak stakes. They date from the mid-1800s.

Collection of early baskets

Plate 17

It is not difficult to find a place to display a basket collection in this converted barn from the mid-1800s. This particular collection was gathered primarily in the Midwest, although many of the baskets probably originated in the East.

Plate 18

The woven buttocks basket at the left was used for carrying small packages, fruits, and vegetables.

Most of the factory-made products feature multicolored, stained oak splits and metal nails or staples that bind the handle to the basket. The plaited example at the right is a utility basket from the early 1900s.

It is exceedingly difficult to assign a specific purpose to a given basket. Few baskets were constructed for a single purpose. An exception to this general rule is the coiled ryegrass baskets that were used in baking.

Painted clam basket, circa 1910

Plate 19

Baskets designed for a specific purpose in one section of the country may be unheard of in another section. A few examples include berry baskets from Michigan, apple baskets from southern Illinois, and large field baskets for freshly picked cotton from the southern states.

The painted clam basket from New England is still another example. If a basket of this type is needed in your collection, you may have to travel to the Maine coast to find it. This particular basket dates from the early 1900s.

The desirability of this basket would largely be destroyed if the original paint were stripped and the basket sanded and repainted.

Directly behind the clam basket is the underside of the buttocks basket featured in Plate 18. Seldom is a name more descriptive of the form it represents than in the buttocks basket.

Wire egg baskets, circa 1920

Plate 20

Wire baskets were largely a development of the factory period beginning in the 1870s. The three baskets in the foreground date from the 1920s and were used for holding eggs.

Wire baskets should show signs of rust, scratches, and other evidence of abuse over the years. In recent years there has been a series of reproductions marketed in kitchen and gourmet shops. In time, these reproductions will take on the appearance of being old. Generally, the wire in these later baskets is of a heavier gauge than in the earlier examples.

Elmer Fedder, a contemporary basketmaker from Winchester, Illinois, made the chicken basket shortly before his retirement at the age of 90 in 1966.

Hanging egg basket of split, circa 1840

Plate 21

The hanging split basket was used in gathering eggs and is in remarkably good condition considering the abuse it has received. It appears to have been painted with brown paint at some time. This is a unique basket form that could possibly be European in origin.

The split oak basket with the butter prints is a more conventional basket form that dates from the late 1800s. It too was an egg basket.

The buttocks basket and the rye basket are more standard forms. Note the single-wrapped rim on the buttocks basket, and compare it to the double-wrapped basket rims discussed previously. The break in the top coil of the rye basket offers additional insight into the construction of this basket form.

Rare kidney basket

Plate 22

One of the most significant and uncommon baskets in this book is this kidney basket. Made of split oak by a master basketmaker in the mid-1800s, it was used to transport surprisingly heavy loads. The double-wrapped handle is securely fastened to the basket by pieces of split. This double wrapping of hickory was designed to strengthen the basket.

There is a great deal of regionalism in the names used to describe basket forms. This particular basket, for example, might be called a kidney, buttocks, or gizzard basket.

Apple drying basket, circa 1860

Plate 23

The large rectangular basket with the plaited bottom was used for drying fruit, particularly apples. The cores of apples were removed and slices were placed in a warm area of the house to dry. Dried apples were a staple in puddings, pies, cakes, and snacks during the winter months.

Drying baskets may be found with or without attached handles and in a variety of sizes. Commercial drying baskets are considerably larger than this example. This handcrafted basket measures 18 by 24 inches and is 3 inches deep. It dates from the mid-1800s.

The hanging rye basket has a handle made from a raised coil. This allowed the basket to be hung from a beam when not in use. This rye basket is more tightly coiled and bound than the other rye baskets discussed.

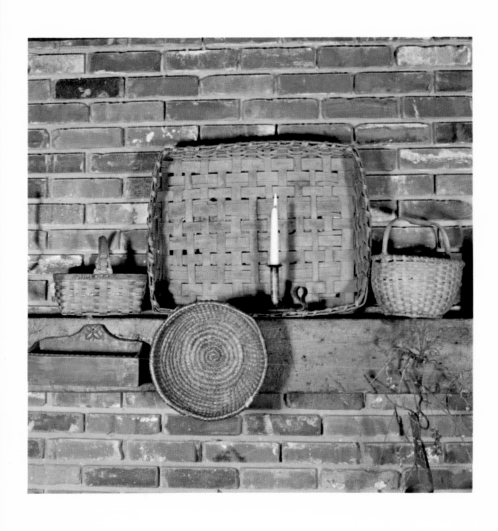

Machine-made split clothes basket, circa 1920

Plate 24

The split clothes basket at the right is typical of the thousands that were produced in the early 1900s. Each piece of split was machine-cut and bears no marks of hand tools. The handles are stapled to the body of the basket. Clothes baskets were usually large because they were designed to hold at least a week's accumulation of dirty clothes. The later wicker clothes hampers were smaller because wash days were closer together.

Clothes baskets were not a product of the factory period. They were handcrafted for many years prior to the development of complex basketmaking machinery. Oval clothes baskets similar to the goose down storage basket in Plate 10 and rectangular, handcrafted split baskets were common early forms.

Early cheese or curd basket